Origins

Yum!

Monica Hughes

OXFORD
UNIVERSITY PRESS

Food

Do you like these foods?

ice cream

mashed potato

tomato salad

orange juice

risotto

corn on
the cob

3

Milk

I like milk.

Milk comes from cows.

What is made from milk?

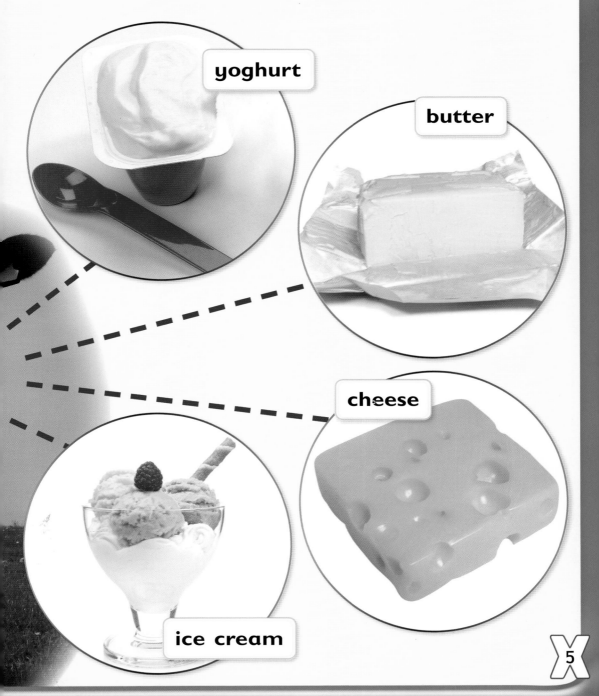

yoghurt

butter

cheese

ice cream

Oranges

I like oranges.

Oranges grow on trees.

What is made from oranges?

orange juice

lolly

sweets

marmalade

Tomatoes

I like tomatoes.

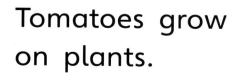

Tomatoes grow on plants.

What is made from corn?

corn on the cob

cornflakes

popcorn

corn soup

13

Potatoes

I like potatoes.

Potatoes grow under the ground.

What is made from potatoes?

crisps

mashed potato

chips

hash browns

What are these foods made from?

tomato salad

marmalade

rice pudding

butter

crisps

cornflakes